T0147455

Shadows, Mirrors, Pearls

Shadows, Mirrors, Pearls

LESLIE JOHNSON

iUniverse, Inc.
New York   Bloomington

Shadows, Mirrors, Pearls

iUniverse books may be ordered through booksellers or by contacting:

iUniverse
1663 Liberty Drive
Bloomington, IN 47403
www.iuniverse.com
1-800-Authors (1-800-288-4677)

ISBN: 978-1-4401-8403-1 (sc)
ISBN: 978-1-4401-8404-8 (ebk)

Printed in the United States of America

iUniverse rev. date: 05/13/2010

To My Family

Table of Contents

Poetry

I did

They looked up to him
Him whose words and music came in from the radio
    about you and me
So I dressed up real pretty in muslin
and I died
they came again
louder with rhythm
and I died
new lyrics
should be the title of his next CD

…speak about her and me with compassion.

The Wind I Saw

A fierce wind
You would say
That one came in March or last year
But not this one
It's one you can't imagine
But I can

First it stormed then it raged
Mother Nature
In front of my house
One early afternoon
And she came in so strong the cardinal on the fence whirled
To prevent herself from falling
Nor did she fly off
She seemed to know the sky was no place for her now
This same wind so distressed a tree
That there arose a sweeping sound from its branches
And the cat beneath the tree scrambled off to the hedges
Because he heard the sound of a broom too close to him

Now you may think me carried away
But I sought refuge in the basement
For like the cat I opted for distance
And a way out

I looked out from a window below ground
Fear walked with me
Like an evil doer

The cardinal chirped no message
Her eyes said it in silence
That tall tree protested
As every limb together in unison flung up skyward
Throwing leaves about
And the red bird, now more defiant, too, flew off quickly
Undoubtedly fleeing and fearing
Both the wind and the cat might come again soon

Yet, to this day, I am sometimes dumfounded and unsure
That day and all those things seem so unlikely

…it's been such a long time since I've daydreamed of
    sunny skies.

Under the Rain

I played whist for two hours
and did not win
it was fun though
and my way of letting him show off
because if I didn't let him win
he was too difficult to be with
…my nephew

The Son

Father holds his hand
As they look up at the tall building
Dazzled by the windows
But mostly by the window washers
Those huge windows are mirrors
Creating photos of their faces
For the boy to see

And because he is a boy
And a good one
He insists on cleaning the windows at home
And cries because he can not
And the father can not stop his sobs

The Weekend

camped out alone
because he would not come along
muddy trail
unpredictable storm
thunder all night long
endless wild and weary
a heavy loaded rifle

Impossible Rooms

while alone
and with my gun
and lost in the low dusk-light
my thoughts turned to doors, halls and walls
these angles and lines were
my pink walls and sheets at home
in my room
I assured myself
without curtains or shawl
for like anyone who wanted something more
my demands required attention
from old favorite songs came
words from his letters
I whispered them aloud until my memory faded
and they became silly murmured words.

hours later
nothing stirred but silence
that drove the lightening bugs away from their homes
suggesting happiness
in the sky flying together

at midnight, still I could not sleep
the rooms returned
so I counted them
one, two, three…
until the door inched forward slowly and finally closed

sleep, incredulous sleep

Mirrors Like Theirs

Tough I called, they didn't come
But there comes a time for kindnesses
And in the morning of my greatest cry and doubt that
    divided us
From white lilies, voices sang
Until they came, one, two… twelve

Joy I knew when
Two perfumed lovely young twins
Gave me mirrors
In the first, I saw my face
And in the second one
I could see the following day
Oh, betray me not
Sweet tranquil tomorrow.

Tomorrow

Looking forward
To the passing of another day
And feeling good
Being careful for nothing
Because there's still time.

LOVE IS…

love means it's never over
you are again as yesterday
and long ago, as always
a dream i prayed and
God responded
binding us
we are one
sincerely and forever

Love…

love will find a way…forgiveness

Around the Pump

disaster…but couldn't it be a little worse
waiting, hurried and worried but not just for gas
truly hoping the credit card purchase is approved

long lines…while a man leans against the pump
his face is like a groom's (a frown as a groan escapes his lips).

Livin' Love

We are the women and children
You promised to love forever more
And unto death do us part
Remember our faces and eyes
As the faint echoes of our voices remind you
Far off and away-where you now are
Husbands, fathers and brothers
Men who love their country and families
And serve in Iraq.

High Steps

someone told me to leave the hotel bar
the dust is streaming along the curb
I can't see my feet
I've lost my way
roaming and walking in my sleep
because I don't know the way home.

THE RIVERS OF SURGING WATERS

black people are colors
uncles aunts cousins brothers and sisters
that hurt him like the oppressors
you are merciless and can not see
because you call him light-skinned
he no longer wants to live
but lives on behind bars
deep in the valley

and beyond recognition

WHO

who is saying nothing about ending war
accepting public opinion and indecision
and ignoring God's
ill fortune ruin and death
until we kneel and whimper
on streets and in closets
yes on our knees
waiting and watching in darkness

Autumn

Apples
deer
frost
a pumpkin patch
so charming to lovers
but the dull eyes of the drunken
see a twisted shape at evening

he remembers nothing or
remembers too late
because of a ludicrous habit.

Daughters of My Friends

Twelve veiled women
Came to dinner
And though stately, I had my doubts

The twelfth one lingered in my imagination
Beyond my reach, but addressing and beckoning to me
Though intelligible, so many clever words made me dizzy

Unlike me, not to understand or remember
But yet their fun didn't seem an unkindness
So I would be surprised to never see them again.

BY MY HEELS

The way is often darkened
In the night the quiet squeaks
And there is no hope
For a life's rewards fade to nothing
Confusion produces no good thing
I agonize morning day and night
No answers emerge
Separated and ailing
I retreated to my dreams
For conversations with the skeleton
That rises from the human and animal bones
All dressed up in gold and silver
With the unfolding of his arms
I see the faces of others around me
Worse than calf's liver
Screams and stench make me queasy
So large a group
Is this my fate?

CELEBRATION

like an evil curse is guilt
close your eyes
say be gone
regret no longer follows like a shadow
in this lush field
rejoice

…keep the flies away

THE OTHER SPEAKS

…another state of consciousness
wide awake
unable to speak
yet sound is there
deep inside and far away
in distress like a spell
tangled silver and black flashes
serpents fire and smoke
so lucid that reality passed away
an extraordinary place

EVERY TIME I SLEEP

he comes
one like no other
and what a surprise
he is mine
and makes me wonder
why a dream and
this place where
no one watches
among my thoughts and desires
and despite my best efforts
all fades at day light
…I am sleep walking and talking to the sky

ROAD TO A VICTIM

they live on the corner and on the street
and know long days and nights
little quiet or sleep
children along the way
beg for food
they offer sex for money
and prefer to go home with strangers
and do not cry

JOHNNY PORCH GLIDER

watch them line up
for the latest album
by johnny porch glider
the pop rock artist and con man
who wrote that bumper sticker
"no man seeks character or dignity
where there's all this free damn ass"

Carefree City

In the light of day
Taxis and cars line the streets
People crowd the sidewalks
Hail buses and trains
On their way to work
Reading the daily paper

Standing on the corner
Passing time, words and wisdom
About the editor who writes about the city
It is great and can not fail
He tells the world and
An audience large and educated
But they do not challenge his truths
Until the lie is discovered and
The editor goes to court

But to judge and jury he won't testify
Million dollar attorneys keep him safe
And make fools of the people and the city

Hear it again
Fame money and connections
Payoffs and greedy men

WRETCHED PEOPLE

my ex-husband

my boss's ex-wives and ex-mistresses

SHE

if he never calls or comes to visit

then she should soon stop thinking

about what might have been

she won't forget...

the drugs

his crimes

their crying children

and the death penalty

THE WOMAN

the men talked
about black madness
neck chains bangles and her ankle bracelet
and despite the danger
they desired her
and hoped

TILA

Her face is the color of soot

her hair is short and nappy

she is the child-mother of a son

and her name is Tila Mae Amin

and she should have no shame

because isn't it right that you

should love her

instead of hating her with those

cold killing stares

and curse words

a mother's daughter

a young daughter with a daughter

Mom Died

...guess what I found...an eight piece canister set, my great-grandmother's wedding pictures, costume jewelry and make up

...a night gown I gave her over thirty years ago

...diamonds, opals and pearls

...her auburn wig

Steps to the Pasture

...I couldn't let these moments pass without saying,
    Mother Dear
How fondly remembered are your steps and the quiet
As is your gaze in spring at fences that needed mending

Near...like in often remembered dreams
But now transformed into magnificence, too
You will be for the rest of my life
Until that day when I will know where you are and be
    there with you in an instant
Away from among the rocks to the pealing bells in
    pastures and the gray-light dawn.

BEFORE DAYLIGHT

I saw them before daylight out there

Among the weeds cans and bottles

A black dog and a white cat walked together

At the corner they met a contemplating skunk

Now the dog and cat begged and pleaded

Don't ruin it for us

Birds overhead his promise and they sang

Trees listened

Even a squirrel joined the crowd

And I ran after them

But they ran faster

Their words faded to whispers

And I can't tell you

A thing about their wit

THE LION ROARED

the young lion roared

because at the river's bank

he saw her face

remembered from his days as a cub

she trembled to hear his fierce appeal

and up the nearest tree she fled

where she hid and watched him eat lunch, hoping food
would make him sleep

breathlessly waiting on a limb

with the sun high in the sky

he lowered himself to the ground and slept

she crept down and escaped

and ran so fast through the clover patch she lost the
cherished lucky amulet

given as a present by her mother

who had once been a great and famous circus lioness

when she arrived home in tears

her mother listened and cried too

now he awoke to find that she had sneaked away

and sought her in the forest without success

but he found the lucky charm upon a path

and took it for himself

he placed it around his neck and

immediately fell to the ground in a deep sleep

enchanted he dreamed of her

and when he awoke and had eaten some greens

the lion set out for that distant place

but became discouraged

yet sought to see her for one last time

with every step the pain tore at this heart so deeply

that he veered off the road and into a ditch

where he met a toad

now this here toad did what he must do for the broken
    hearted lion; he was not a prince nor a ruler, but a
    cunning croak

who knew about the famous lioness

so he led the lion to the den on the outskirts of town

and upon seeing her gaze sought her for himself

the betrayed lion did not know what to do

neither did the father lion

but mother did

she had dreamed of her daughter's suitor

and knew he would be wearing the lucky charm

so the mother gladly welcomed her son-in-law to be

while the toad hopped off rejected and frustrated

for a lioness could not change his fate

now you may say

this is a simple tale about fate

about youngsters in love or

a toad that needed to stick with his own kind

but i say it's about a mother's love

and there's one more thing you should know

it's about this story's author

who added a message for all lovers

one that extends forever and throughout all eternity

sealed in the heavens and approved by all the Gods

for true lovers who are separated and confused

do not despair

for if in agony you fall asleep

and dream of the lion with the lucky charm

know that your lover shall return to you

and may a curse befall any one

who denies the benevolence of this tale

or dares to tamper with any word or words

that takes away from the author's good intentions

and God's glorious blessing

The Bird Told Me…

when i see a bob-tailed rabbit
i practice landings on its tail

…he talked to a giraffe with a knot in its neck

…about a summer two thousand years ago
there were no ants mosquitoes or flies
and no night at all
…a star is a wonderful place

By The Pond...

did you ever see
a bullfrog do the back stroke...

or see a beaver with a
horse's tail...

Takin' Pictures...

a dog skipping rope while chewing gum...

a cat pitching horse shoes...

a mouse eating cheese and sipping fruit punch...

a camel doing a back bend...

a rhino napping on a whale's back...

baby's foot in her mouth
right beside her thumb and pacifier...

my shoes on my hands...
because that's how my four year old granddaughter painted
a picture titled, "Grandma at the Beach"
my arms are brown and the sneakers are white
and although we are thousands of miles away
I am glad her inner most independence and love forged
a new place for us on the beach.

Fiction

Pieces from Distant Echoes

Around Mirrors

For the late Friday afternoon commute on the slow-moving CTA bus in Chicago, the July heat and the absence of air conditioning spread agitation and insults among passengers who competed for turns to tell about the horrors of riding rush hour city buses in summer. And none more than the bookkeeper in white shirt, navy tie and mirrored clasp. At least that's what Dailey Upton thought while straining to watch out the window as the bus moved along King Drive.

"Big Macs" the school boys called the buses on this side of town where most folks knew something about commuting and riding cheap. A woman slept and reminded Dailey that tired people boarded, pushing and shoving for a place in the aisle. A place for packages and carry-ons; mostly tote bags and blue and yellow shopping bags from Dominick's Stores.

The heat and stale air weighed as much as the bags and packages. And along with it hung dampness so that the new red D-John t-shirt and cap seemed ridiculous purchases. The matching cap that made her brown eyes exciting and not just pleasantly warm no longer seemed like something she had wanted for so long. A cap and shirt that really weren't for her, but purchases the clever sales clerk had talked her into buying. A cap bought for a weekend, though inexpensive but not cheap, soothed some of her nervousness about going home to visit the folks. The only way to explain such an impulsive non-essential purchase at the mall near her apartment. An apartment just minutes away from her job at the finance company and less than fourteen miles from the Southside but the distance seemed greater. Perhaps the long absence and the uneasy feeling made the distance seem further in space and time.

She closed her eyes momentarily to shut out thoughts about going home and sank into the seat as the bus traveled along the cluttered street where drivers honked horns and braked every few feet. "Don't go home," Kim's voice came back, "Just for the weekend. Just because Mill will be home," her thoughts answered Kim's who was known in the office for giving too much advice.

Watching traffic or thinking of nothing was better than thoughts about seeing her younger sister Mill-a cousin legally adopted and therefore her sister. Double kin is what she was. Not pleasant feelings at all, but it was the only way to describe how horrible it felt to know that the prettier, younger Mill loved Tommy. Yes, little sister wanted big sister's boyfriend. And not so long ago, they had all been pals. It had all started as a simple dare. Then it escalated to love that made Dailey want to win his heart. She fought back and won. "So why go home?" Kim had asked, thinking aloud, "Why bother…it was a dare so who cares?"

A weird feeling started inside -in her stomach- and then spread all over. Dailey cared because it was equally horrible to know that Mama and Daddy seemed not to notice or care. Or something! You could call them neutral when Mill had spoken candidly about visiting Tommy at college. Mill could do any thing. Any damned thing!

Mill got what she wanted most of the time. Daddy added a new bedroom just for Mill. There were new curtains, carpet and wall paper. He had given her the room so that she could live at home while attending City College. And just over two years ago for her high school graduation Mill had visited New Your City for spring break. The Atlantic could be seen by visitors eating lunch in huge office buildings. A tour of private gardens and parks filled with blossoming trees and flowers and things seldom seen cost hundreds of dollars.

Dailey told herself it was best to move on and forget. After all everyone expected her to let Tommy go without a fight. To fight and quarrel on and on would mean she was acting like a bitter older sister affected by too much emotion and crying. But despite it all, Tommy had told Mill, "No. There's Dailey."

Mill had stopped but Dailey knew she was waiting.

Such an awful thing and great big mess happened so fast. Dailey couldn't think of anything worse. And didn't know what was the matter with herself. Nor Mill and Tommy. She wanted to do the right thing. Even if it meant letting go. Yes, she felt like that because Daddy had never liked Tommy. She had met him in high school when he was shy and puzzled about life. A tall lanky boy with thick black hair, Tommy told silly stories about his dog, Beans.

"My dog whistles and winks…eats popcorn and sugar pops."

"He's silly," Daddy said.

His silliness and nervousness about daddy was ridiculous, that was his way or imagination but his affection couldn't be ignored. He might have been confident enough to sound funny but Daddy killed it. But later, after hours and hours together making up silly sentences and songs turned into so much fun and laughter. That kind of laughter isn't soon forgotten. And helped them during the grueling days without employment and right up to the day they got hired at the finance company. Good computer skills made it easy to land a job, but it was hard to sign up people for loans. Tommy hated asking people to take out a loan so after working at the company for almost three months, he quit and went off to college in eastern Illinois.

Weeks before the end of the first semester, he changed majors-from English to Elementary Education. "My God, My God," Dailey said when he changed majors again. This time it was coaching. Then finally a guidance counselor convinced him to get a liberal arts degree.

She had cried often but stuck by him because of their love. Daddy had watched and listened night after night. He had heard her sobs and known her frustration. But there could be no mistake about their love. From some place special it had come and it wasn't in the least bit damaged or spoiled. She had lost nothing. But something about not talking nagged at her. Most of the time silence was a gigantic hint and one of her most vivid recollections. She couldn't explain it because daddy was so good at keeping quiet. Like when something happened at the factory years ago that made mom cry. It was the time when another man's wife slapped Daddy. The woman named Mary Angela had done it and he had come home late smelling like liquor. But after the slap he came home promptly from work and mom stopped crying and looking for him. For the hundredth time she wondered about Mill and Tommy. The chattering came back again. "Mill and Tommy. Mill and Tommy. Mill and Tommy."

The driver slowly rounded the corner, turned toward the curb and the bus came to a halt on Drexel Street. As Dailey stepped from the bus the driver mumbled, "Watch your step. Have a nice evening." She thanked him and brushed past boarders standing on the sidewalk. There must have been five to ten of them as she sought a familiar face, thinking the bus stop was less than a block from the house. The air was heavy, so common because of the closeness of the lake. She heard stereos and T.V.'s and saw many cars with blinding headlights. From the lights just in front of her eyes, Mama emerged, hugged her and reminded her that Daddy and Mill hadn't come to the bus stop. The love surged within. Mama, like no one else, she wanted to talk to her.

They talked and walked side by side but were shy with each other. The air was filled with something too difficult to talk about. She had been so wound up about Mill and

Tommy that she didn't realize until now; this visit would be more like being led down a winding trail.

Dailey slowed and lagged behind Mama thinking and counting the foot steps.

She fought back tears regarding the outside of the house. The porch light revealed fair condition and no peeling paint. At the kitchen door entrance, someone who looked like a football player passed without uttering a single word. Could he be angry and yearn for Mill with all his heart? Dailey saw the light in the living room where Daddy and Mill sat watching television. His eyes never left the T.V. when he answered her hello. He lay on the couch absolutely still in front of the T.V. Mill sat in the recliner with a magazine in her lap. The white walls and light made her seem quite pleased with herself.

She wore a lavender cap and t-shirt just like Dailey's. Lilac eye shadow matched lavender and nothing else.

Dailey rushed from the room to the kitchen thinking how happy Mill looked. And because for just an instant seeing her was hard to bear. Daddy looked sad and tired but Mill looked completely relaxed and happy.

Her reaction to what Mill wore was quiet. But she had never been so angry. It would have felt great to stand in front of Mill, turning around and around screaming or laughing. Oh well, don't we look great, she thought and imagined herself pouring ketchup on Mill's cap.

Mama came to Dailey's side. She smiled and looked at Dailey and it was as if she wanted something. And urged her. She did not quite know what for.

"Come on Dailey say something," Mama said in a fix-it mood.

But it was difficult to do. Practically impossible.

Unsure of what to say, Dailey thought of ignoring Mama's urging but answered, "Somethingggggg!" She wanted to get even with Mill but couldn't resist being polite because of Mama. Dailey escaped feeling stupid for not saying what she really wanted to say. Most women would have showed more than just a little resentment and at least a little bit of anger. And some would have been very, very vain. But she knew a little bit about competition and had learned a few lessons very well.

At supper, the checkered table cloth and bright t-shirts made mealtime seem more like a picnic or garden party. Daddy nibbled on fries and didn't seem to care about the fried chicken. He read aloud from the paper about the impending union strike vote and looked more tired.

Mill ate vegetables and drank water. Supper was a snack for her because of some new diet she had learned about from Asi, a nutrition guru at the college. Mill expressed genuine devotion to him.

Dailey hoped she would say something about the "Muscle Man" or the caps and shirts. The waiting seemed to go on forever. Brilliant, admirable Asi grew larger and larger. Exaggerated of course, there might have been a few threads of truth in it.

After supper, it was late enough for bed. Table and dishes belonged to Mama.

Certainly not for daddy. He sought the couch and T.V. Nor were they the kind of chores for Mill, who laughed, walked to the dishwasher and handed her plate to mama before joining daddy in the living room to watch one of those reality shows.

Dailey helped with the cleanup. No part of her wanted to sit, stand and pretend. Helping was easier. She couldn't help feeling that way. And supposed there was nothing to do but keep right on helping and imagining the quiet in the bedroom until it came after helping with the clean-up and listening to mom talk about her catalogs.

Inside, she thought it hadn't changed since she last saw it. It was a small room on the second floor in the rear of the house. An old twin bed and matching chest of drawers stood along the back wall side by side. It would be impossible to find another set like it. Tears swelled and flowed. She lit the candle, turned out the light and lay on the bed fully clothed; thinking no amount of tears would make her feel the way she wanted to feel.

Their faces went around and around in her head for an hour then another. The candle went out. She lit it again thinking of her apartment and the ferns and ivy. It left again after a moment. She wondered could this be true; denying the much entitled light. Forgotten and fumbling for the candle again, her cell phone rang. It was Kim from work sending over a newsletter, ads and even horoscopes. She did it several times a day to co-workers and friends. One straight talking man told her to leave. "The only thing that matters is that you should go."

"Go quickly and quietly," a caller from California said.

"You are being too nice to the bitch."

"Don't blame others for your troubles."

Dozens of messages were on the phone, from vacation tips to ads for i-pods, free coupons and boxes of cereal. Sadly one number for removing phone numbers from solicitors' lists was included. Some of the far-fetched ones told about doing sexy things.

She deleted many of them. And stored others-like the one for removing phone numbers from lists and the one that promised to send greetings to Mill's phone number immediately upon request, using not so nice words, of course. She wanted to record something clever but couldn't do it. Instead she gathered up her things and left on tip-toes. At the entrance to the kitchen a light came in from the window and Mill's cap came into view on the table. Taking it seemed easy and right, she thought stuffing it in her bag with obvious pleasure.

As she left, it seemed that Daddy and Mama called out, "Dailey."

Outside a crowd waited at the bus stop. A man sat on the curb drinking beer. A couple argued. Jazz music played, but not good Jazz. It sounded like squeaky music from a $39.99 ghetto blaster.

She reflected and guessed they would think she acted impulsively. Mama would cry and Daddy would be dumbfounded. Mill would call and leave messages on her machine wanting to know something and not wanting to wait.

Dailey stepped quickly filled with the boldness that surpassed anything she'd ever known before. And felt no pegs in her stomach because at least it would be difficult for them to ignore what she'd done. And what she'd done had been huge and unforgettable, especially because it was what she truly wanted to do and exactly the thing to make Mill unhappy for a long, long time.

Early Morning Kind

Above Chicago standing on the "L" Platform waiting for the train fifty feet from the expressway speeding drivers never noticed me or the life-sized billboard photo of an eighteen year old wearing a yellow bikini and sipping coke. Two men several feet away waiting stared at the pretty woman holding the bottle to her lips. They admired her belly button in voices loud enough for me to hear and called her, "Princess". Other pretty faces and bodies told beautiful stories on bus panels, cab trunks and bumpers, but none compared to the Princess'. It seemed that she understood them.

I saw Jimmy up there New Year's Day among the paper roses and tulips exactly three months before my fortieth birthday while seated on a train at 5 a.m. heading for Chicago's Southside. Few passengers boarded because the transit authority observed a holiday schedule which meant making all stops. A ride that normally took forty-five minutes now took nearly two hours to complete. All stops were too many stops for most people on a day when it seemed so right to go faster-and not slower. But it was a city-wide imposed holiday schedule and I was tired, but glad to be going home after a night of working a North Shore party with my cousin Ciel, a maid to a wealthy Chicago Jewish family named, Packards. Ciel, my favorite cousin and the only one in Chicago looked out for me and that's why the opening was tendered to me; "Anna is my cousin and she'll do just fine," Ciel explained to Mrs. Jackie Packard, the hostess and her employer.

She meant you'd better not do one damned thing to mess this up. And the Packards paid well and that helped me, a college student who existed with little money for food, housing, clothing and just about any other thing. Seventy-five dollars for five hours of work was pretty good for me and so I felt fine or at least okay about working five hours for the seventy-five.

Maybe fine showed all over my face or perhaps it was the fact that I had only three more stops before reaching my exit at Bailey Street. Two more stops to go and less than ten minutes apart. The third stop would take almost thirty minutes-the last one and well worth waiting for, thoughts of leaving the train filled me with anticipation. Just going home, and just a little bit weary of working the dinner party, combined to remind me how much I had wanted the party to end. The money in my pocket would go to the bank for my night class in literature at the local junior college. Tired but happy about paying for an African drama class in the future made me feel my efforts were meaningful. Kind of like getting out of the way of the rapidly opening and closing train doors.

I watched the door open at the Loop Station. A small mass of tired faces rushed through. One who entered last was a black man. He saw me when I saw him. What brown eyes stared into my darker brown ones and immediately I wanted to be some place else. What had we done right on the train surrounded by people? He approached me after such a hard night's work and there he was, "What's your name?" he said sitting down beside me searching my eyes and face before I could turn away. What was coming into my life? "Don't ignore me, tell me your name."

"Yeah?" I knew he would demand much from me. He looked too good not to.

"That's what I said! What do you want me to do, take it from you? I asked your name."

I looked at him, forced a grin because he was far too good looking not to deserve politeness even though his good looks seemed to say you don't ever waste courtesy on my kind of man. At least that's what I thought sitting there beside him, shoulder to shoulder.

He persisted, unwilling to take the quiet smile and no for an answer. "Just your name?" He asked loud enough to attract the attention of other riders who now understood he wanted my name. They listened to him explain his early departure from the home of a sick uncle. His story was sad, especially on New Years'.

One man rose for the next stop. My stop was after his. I knew what to do, had told myself a hundred times. He reached over and placed a business card in my hand. His fingers reminded me of the keyboard man's from my computer class but they seemed softer and warmer. My silence had gotten me his name. What could I do but whisper my name apologizing for having to climb over him so suddenly for the next stop and telling him how sorry I was about his uncle before walking hurriedly through the door. He shouted words as the train sped off; Jimmy said, "Good-bye, Anna."

Later, I called the number on his business card only to find out it was his uncle's barber shop. So I left a message including my name, phone number and lots of details about school, and even my address. And the next day I saw him at the station waiting to accompany me to school before going to work at his uncle's shop on the west side near Roosevelt Road and Halstead, a neighborhood well known to tourists, but one I knew little about. Let's face it in a city the size of Chicago, there were always places to be discovered.

And that was how it got started; this thing between us that lots of people called love. It was good sometimes as the story goes, sometimes things got bad because both of us had past memories of bad former lovers. There were so many things that impeded our life together. I felt strongly about kindness and cleaning around the house but not Jimmy. And his reasons about not being kind were that it was impossible most of the time, and besides little kindnesses weren't his style. "Housekeeping isn't something you should stop doing," Jimmy wouldn't give an inch. The more I did it the more he liked not doing it because I could do it better.

"It's down right stupid most of the time...some of the time, yeah cause it just doesn't exist the rest of the time." He argued nonsensibly about his feelings about what it meant. I clearly understood that some things couldn't exist all the time or even most of the time. And after that

I heard about ten of his co-workers and friends who were single, mean and insensitive because of bad relationships. On he went about the past rooted in bad memories. He explained it. Whatever it was! Jimmy's substitute for love was "it". Or perhaps it was his triumph over love or something.

So for two and a half years I settled for it, the man I wanted to run away from; the one I didn't want to marry. The one man who truly meant so much that it was difficult to think about another man. Call it devotion or stupidity. I had to stand my ground and I did it well enough to keep it together squeezing out something for a few years. Occasionally he would spend a weekend away from me but that was once every six months or so. But nothing about his distractions made me lose my temper and I figured every woman was trying to catch a man including Jimmy.

We spent Sundays together. That was our special day and it was our day for talking before the next work week. So on Sunday I learned to heed his words, thoughts and feelings. Although sometimes the conversation wasn't pleasant because he told me too much; stuff about the biker gangs in the old neighborhood; stuff that I just didn't want to hear. But after more than two years together, most of the time I listened to every sordid word of the story and learned to anticipate the violence he recounted.

Gangs became a signal from him about things he didn't want to do but had to do in the old section of the city with old friends who lived in a perishing neighborhood. What would a man his age be doing with gangs? That should have been the last thing on his mind. I faded as the violence increased and exploded. What did I need to know but didn't want to know? He talked about the old neighborhood. It only happened on Sundays and could be endured for one day. After hearing him out on Sunday, my thoughts of the next day's class assignments took me away quickly enough. The week ahead filled me with anticipation and swept me away from something that couldn't be changed.

Leaving on Monday morning, my eyes traveled back and away from the door to him sitting on the couch watching "Good Morning, America". It was routine, I thought, despite the mention of gangs on Sunday. The two of them, Jimmy and the old neighborhood seemed so far away. I didn't say good-bye. That was something I never did when leaving. Besides it was Government Monday, one of those days when the buses were half empty because city and state employees only worked half a day to save the taxpayers money and that meant I didn't need to hurry. But I always needed to hurry among these people in this city. My feet felt heavy, in a slow morning mood of their own. I tried to control them and my temper as grinning cab drivers sought my attention, "Honey, you can ride today for half price. Don't you want to ride with me today?" The Government Mondays made them lose money and they said anything to attract riders.

Returning home eight hours later, after class, the library and working four hours braiding hair at The Community Service Center, I saw and half-listened to Mr. Green, our neighbor who asked me about Jimmy. I read him. He wanted to know something about something. I knew an angle when I heard one and reminded myself that Green gossiped too much for reasons I'm not really sure of.

Less than two hours later, I was interrupted by a loud pounding at my door.

"Miss Anne Gail W___, we're from the detective division, open up."

"Do you have a warrant?" was the only thing I could mutter. Detectives at my door! What would the neighbors think? What did I think?

"We want to talk to you, mame. I understand you're a friend of Jimmy Kelsley's?

Is that right?"

At the mention of Jimmy's name, I opened the door but didn't release the safety chain, just like on T.V. The men wore immaculate black suits, flashed shiny badges and they wanted to talk.

"What about Jimmy?" I knew Mr. Green listened, heard his radio playing because the door stood ajar.

"We want to talk to you. Will you let us come in... it'll take just a few minutes."

"It must be a mistake." I fought back fear but removed the safety chain. No smile showed on their shaven faces and my shaking hands revealed my emotions; they carried pistols in their shoulder belts.

"We hate bothering you, mame." The taller one explained following me. I sank into the big chair and the two of them sat on the couch. The taller one crossed his ankles while the other detective crossed his legs. "We got a call that Jimmy was missing and wondered when you last saw him."

"Was he here today?" the second man almost interrupted.

"Yes," I nodded knowing that Jimmy hadn't been missing for more that a few hours. So why were they here asking me questions. It was obvious that someone wanted to know about Jimmy. Someone had called the police.

"Have you spoken to him since you saw him? Have you tried to call him? We know he'd want to speak to you." They led me on with questions that told little to someone untrained and unfamiliar with the authority and regiment of those who worked day and night in law enforcement-and confused most citizens. They concealed and revealed nothing. I stammered, unable to control my fear and emotions, "We talk during the day most of the time, but not today."

"It's very unfortunate...he was in a fire and couldn't get out," the taller one said rising. "But with the gangs, we never know. They are always staging something, but seldom is it this bad...the fire, mame..."

He said it because of my streaming, uncontrollable tears about the homicide. I remembered nothing; leaving for school, working or opening the door for these men, I thought as the tall man started.

"We're sorry...if you hear any thing, please give us a call." He handed me a card and walked out.

At the sound of the closing door, screams escaped uncontrollably. A fire caused this and what could I do but wonder how and why? How could the living fight with the gangs and their dead? And what about his uncle and family? How could I talk to them. Ask them about Jimmy's past again.

"Jimmy," I whispered, not remembering his face but his shadow in front of the T.V. just this morning. I couldn't and wouldn't remember him. My memories were of his socks and clothing. The things I pleaded with him about-cleaning up and all that. The shirts he loved. He didn't have many and seldom wore the expensive ones. He preferred jeans and t-shirts and had dozens of them. Like a good many men, Jimmy left them hanging over the back of a chair in the bedroom and seldom hung them up. I had told him to do it before leaving for school. He was stubborn, but he'd done it.

The room was neat; the bed was made.

I rose hurriedly seeking the truth in our closet. It was ours and something we shared. I stood there frozen, just couldn't move-Jimmy's clothing was gone. He'd left a bat, some dirty sneakers and half-a-dozen t-shirts which meant he was alive and cheating again. No, he's with Stick, I told myself as visions of his new interest invaded my head. Stick was an old friend and former roommate who liked being divorced and girls with exotic condoms.

I thought of sleep but everything hurt like my head. It wasn't the first time a guy and this guy had done something stupid. And Jimmy had done this before, with the gangs and all, it was his second time. Hardly breathing, I waited for the phone to ring. Time passed. Suddenly the damned thing rang and I couldn't move. It went on for about thirty seconds.

He has the nerve, I thought, knowing Jimmy had called. That girl had probably left him or better still, kicked him out and he'd called me in desperation. But nothing rubbed me the wrong way like the competition for his love. I hated anyone who would dare interfere-a hate for any woman or Stick Man.

"Guess what! So what!" I whispered, knowing he would call again. He wasn't gone yet. Without the girl he would now feel a tremendous void. And without me he'd know how stupid he acted. I left the couch for the bedroom. It felt strange without him. I swore and dried tears thinking of the girl and the other time when he'd come back within a day and called the police to confirm a false report. I felt stunned-it had happened again.

But she, the other woman was around, some where and waiting. She probably had two or three friends telling her what to do and say to him-and to me indirectly.

I understood. I'd answer, not yell or hang up the next time he called. Men like Jimmy enjoyed and remembered the good times. When an argument got started because of his selfishness that drove him to leave, then the other woman made her mistake-of course, sooner or later and without the benefits of the good memories and that would send him packing, unable to subject himself to her whims and demands, never so soon.

Because of the memories, I would get my man back and maybe a ring if I wanted it. At 3:00 a.m., the phone rang. He explained, "Stick wanted to borrow some clothes." He apologized about the gangs using his name. It was the way they did things and ended it, "I'm sorry it happened. It won't happen again." He promised. By 4:30 I walked out the door to meet him for breakfast, and the other woman was the past. There had once been a time to let go. But it had been long ago when I'd first let him come back. But not now. And not yet. Because the other woman was out there waiting and confused by the silence. And hopefully she would loathe every dizzying second.

Curlicues

Abbey, my daughter took clothes from the dryer to the upstairs bedroom for folding and packing. I sat watching at the window as my granddaughter Terri played outside in the front yard. Watching Abbey was never easy but she has packed hundreds of times. The sound of the clock and refrigerator drowned out her voice. What was she muttering? My hands shivered in my lap but I couldn't help her now. My hands won't do it now. Not just yet. The thought of my precious Terri leaving made me sad. It was hard to think about being her age and to remember learning to tie the ribbons on my beginner ballet slippers. Wearing my scalloped chiffon skirt was easiest and like getting all dressed up for a party. I even wore it while sleeping and in my dreams where the light of day shined like a fourteenth-floor hall in a tall office building. Up on my toes, above everyone, I jumped like the ballerina on T.V. Well not exactly like her, she jumped much higher. At five years old the pretty lady dressed in a pink tutu and white tights looked pretty amazing.

The attic on Sunday afternoons after dinner was center stage and where my dance steps turned into curlicues; an unusual name for the elegance of a ballerina but the word came from my imagination and it described the special dance steps on the slopes flying high above trees and river banks where time became a long song and dance in a strong wind that made the music louder. All I needed was to hear the music, see lace curtains, lanterns and white fences. Voices spoke from the curtains, and encouraged me, "Dance, Molly, dance."

My first dance imitated the pretty ballerina's. But only the first one, because my second dance was all my own. I learned my lessons often on the verge of sleep from too much apple pie at dinner and aching to play outside instead of the attic. The dance was new and different and shouldn't be spoiled by old habits. The high clouds and a long wide road seemed to go on for ever. The end seemed so far away until my flying horse came quickly. No one had ever told me a horse could fly.

"They canter," Mrs. Richman, the kindergarten teacher had explained to the class.

The horse sang as we traveled to a pasture where he had a home and family. Their pounding hearts ended our journey and my heart pounded back, louder, faster and sadder. The hands on my wristwatch weren't for now but for another time. Nothing made sense but jumping and pivoting. It was hard to think straight alone and without my horse.

At first, the wind lifted me, hastily the calm energy of its way prevailed. What couldn't be exciting about such an encounter? But soon fantasies and happiness met the sunset and the road became a forest. Such a place of great joy and beauty or so I thought, but nature surprised especially surrounded by a forest-wouldn't you think? Soon after came rain. I wished for a blanket and heard the sound of the stranger who lived there. Shadows surrounded after the rain. His sound gripped firmly. So great was its dreadful sound like a thing returned from the grave seeking a home or food. Light came in from its half shut eyes as the bear came closer.

I couldn't speak, jump or pivot but my flailing arms and legs propelled me. Savage and hardened, but compelled closer, it ran faster so as to apprehend me with those paws that looked like big peacock's feet. He couldn't leave the forest and endure the gaze of my parents. Nor would the attic be a source of great joy; not like the forest at all. At least, that's how I've always thought about it.

Years later, it seemed so wrong that bears and little girls couldn't play. Not peek-a-boo or nothing. Looking back it all seemed not so long ago and unfair. The thoughts gave me a queasy feeling in my stomach and reminded me that within a few hours the house would be empty again. My stomach told of too much silence and loneliness. But it had to happen. They had to leave for home. Ted wanted them home by the end of the day and his request shouldn't be resented. Dear Ted loved them as much as I did.

Unhappy with nothing else to do, I cut cake, poured coffee for myself and a glass of milk for Terri and called out to her. The wet sponge met the counter top, up and down and round and round without grace.

Unlike magic, and undistinguished.

Under the Sun

After my twenty-five year marriage ended in divorce, I slammed the door behind me and buried myself in yellow blossoms on a canvas. Of relevance to my own attitude, strange images filled my dreams, and daydreams with a brush in my hand. There faces and the places were unknown, visited infrequently, liked intensely because of the beautiful colors, but not loved. Not about love at all, or so it seemed. But the place had been there all the time.

I needed art and knew it helped me get away from myself to ease my guilt about my own life and my adult children. Both daughters had marriages that had gone on for far too long; not pursuing divorce could only be a warning to the half-living, half-married. Vows didn't mean spending happy evenings together. And my son, Ron, lived in the local village, instead of with his wife Emma, and their four year old daughter, Terri. The Village, he insisted was like sleeping in a forest at morning or evening because of the band on the stage. Like from below ground, in man holes, a view he'd seen for over twenty years of work. My analogy and one he refuted.

Beneath the earth was a hard way to earn a living, I reminded myself while driving to my art class far away from The Village accompanied by my granddaughter who preferred spending the day with me to going to the stage surrounded by music and grown ups. She might have truly chosen the art over me, but both did her good and noteworthy stuff like that gave me satisfaction.

At the art center, I introduced my darling and sat her down with acrylic paints and paper. Byron, the best-fastest artist and photographer had already turned out three 8 1/2 by 11 sketches and drew a picture of a clown for her. She quickly filled in reds and yellows to embellish his countenance. His smile grew wider and redder. She grinned and nearly matched his toothless smile.

Lana, the best artist in the group had arrived an hour or so earlier and was involved in finishing a fan. That's what she did between portraits and landscapes.

"I'll do anything to finish today," Lana said. She wore a red and black woven scarf around her head. That meant it was time for the salon. Nerves and groans.

"You'll finish well… a masterpiece," I chided, knowing it wasn't her best day. Needing a perm or something like that could make you miserable.

"I don't like it." She answered. "But I don't like the country one either."

"You don't like 'em 'cause they're not done yet…or sold." Sold meant I was spreading enthusiasm. She had made something out of nothing so many times and done it in less time it took me to sketch my doll's faces-dolls with angelic faces made me feel something. Trying to understand why was like trying to understand people. I wondered about the faces while sketching them and left behind my cares for the circles and lines. If through this special, special time defined something for me or in me.

I believe the yellow faces are like daffodils in the sun for me, beckoning and always shining, illustrious and never retreating. I painted my face.

The classes brought me close to several interesting artists. Some stayed. Others came, and left quickly. One had promised to come back. Mel had promised to return for Christmas and it was now February. My face grew tense from inner turmoil; something that could only be changed by time or patience or both. Where was my girl today? Her face hid from me. She walked away. I opted for another time. Ready to leave, I walked to the back of the room for Terri and stiffened. Where could she be? Not in the corner, I thought and wrung my hands. The paints and paper were gone. No paper. Not on the floor, not crumpled beside her chair and it struck me like something terrible.

Fear and shock came. Nothing in this room revealed her whereabouts. I knew she had gone and cursed in silence but couldn't say anything more. Like hell, is how I felt as Lana stepped in front of me. Not Terri but Lana. A face not needed when my personal hell betrayed me. The panic struck me like a stretching, tumbling wall. I stumbled like in rain and landed on the floor behind Byron's chair. In trouble, because of Terri and the fall, Lana apologized, but denied my wish to stand. She insisted, "Stay down. I'll get help."

"Oh, no it's silly," I came back, looking up and noticing Byron's sketches of Terri. He never got bored and sketched until the end of the day or the end of the story.

She shouted back, "Don't be stubborn now. I'll get an ambulance. No, I mean the police."

Terri was fine, I knew that. Byron's sketches told me she was okay. Terri and the clown came first and then they both appeared in Byron's street scene with Emma.

"Oh, no you don't," I screamed, watching Clara the art instructor approaching me from the right with an oxygen bottle and pillows. Crossing to my left, she lowered herself to within an inch of my eyes. "It was Terri," I rattled off trying to explain, watching her make a fuss about me. Me who finally felt no fear if that was truly possible from the floor where no one seemed to understand. They didn't get it. What could be done about unrelenting friends and oxygen? Screams and curses.

Safe and on the other side of the mask, I followed a voice inside my head. One never heard before. Looking on, Byron, beside my pillow, not sketching, and Lana asking me my name repeatedly-and other questions. Her lips moved, "Can you hear me?"

Clara started again, "Your name." They spoke at the same time, "Say it!" No point. I saw photos of Terri with Emma. Byron had got a shot of Emma taking Terri away. Another picture showed her in the Jeep waving good bye.

I had been day-dreaming when Emma arrived to take Terri shopping.

Up went my hair, Lana pushed another pillow beneath my head. Clara's voice sounded louder and she stared sternly. Byron's too-long beard tickled my chin but he affirmed, "She said her name."

Surrounded and on the floor the words and voices sounded like polite meaningless conversation from sleep.

Clara shouted to my face. "What are the primary colors?"

"Answer the question!"

At the crucial moment, I said, "Red, yellow and blue!"

From down there Byron picked me up. With my feet on the floor, "Hello," I said with sheepish reconciliation. I can hear myself talk; can hear them too and I like it.

Lana sighed, "She is okay, at last."

Standing ended the vulnerable feeling. Walking ended all doubts. I thanked them, giving too much attention to it because they'd given me too much. Just like they should have done. Outside the late morning echoes from birds returned just like an early song speaking to me. It felt wonderful to know they shared and had not kept the song to themselves.

Chasing Voices – When the Rain Came

The Widow's Storm

Mrs. Mary Bell Dean, affectionately known as the widow since the recent loss of her husband of fifty years, Braid, seemed to be confronting a few new challenges. The least of which was the gossip circulating about her marriage at the age of fifteen when most young ladies went seeking consent to attend a Saturday evening dance.

No, the gossip about her marrying too young, though successfully, couldn't match recent developments about the love between the widow's daughter, Rose and the handsome young officer, Jerry, who worked for the local tourist commission of the state of Tennessee.

The beautiful gardens and parks had caught the young Jerry Bender's eye while still a youth. The sunny, lush area and the three parks attracted visitors both near and far. The two lakes (the Row and the Long) one river (the Main) spread and fell into the nearby Atlantic Ocean.

Those Benders, as they were often referred to collectively, knew a good reputation in the community because of the elder deacon, Roger Bender. As deacon, his family and affairs in the community received the attention of the earnest and insincere kind. Most church members and citizens meant no harm-but some discussions seemed appalling because the town's people knew about the young Jerry, but the widow did not; because as some had duly noticed, it had to do with what she hadn't been paying attention to. And nobody wanted to tell the widow. They talked about it behind her back, only hinting about her daughter and the man she hoped to marry.

Roger Bender or Deacon B was Jerry's father and had helped most people in the county with farming and just about anything around the house. He also helped with land deeds, taxes and projects like the community water authority. Water projects brought in money so he had earned lots of respect and that's why the just about to happen talk caused a stir. And came right up to the church and was told by a would be suitor rejected far too often and one that had run off from at least a half-dozen or so prospects. A man known for walking about Long Shore flirting with young ladies and making 'em nervous so much so that if a young lady whispered, "He made me nervous" all who overhead the whisper or rumors immediately knew that Ivan Jones had been about annoying the young ladies. But not today, he was talking to Deacon B and the deacons; telling it about Jerry. Telling it because that's what he did and because bad weather had been forecasted. The kind of stormy weather that kept most from venturing too far away. Staying close and talking just because. But not a young man in love like Jerry, who had headed to the Dean house despite the forecast and aimed to talk to the widow about getting married.

Just about the time Ivan Jones stood there talking in front of the church because of the storm warning,

Jerry sat down in the Dean kitchen for soup, bread and discussion. The lovely Rose sat across from him at the opposite end of the table, sipping water and eating bread. She thought only of obtaining permission to marry and knew the matter would be difficult for her mother. Life was lonely now. Death burdened both mother and daughter. Asking mother to marry made her feel guilty. Her mind went numb. She wasn't there, far away from her mother behind a curtain listening and uneasy. At least that's where she was for the first round of words.

Jerry spoke, but took no delight in asking, "I've been wanting to take Rose to the other side of the lake where I bought a house. And I hope you will agree-we belong together and should be married." He stopped before finishing his planned proposal, smiling and hoping his point had been made because it was why he had come and what he aimed to do.

Mary Bell Dean looked away from the hand on hers she'd been staring at and looked right into Jerry's eyes. "Do you mean in a storm? Hardly possible and most unlikely. Not for a few days; may be weeks or months because that's how it is in these terrible, terrible storms." Her heart pounded with joy. She need not say no or even risk making Rose unhappy because the horrible weather threatened more than a mother ever could or nearly as much. That's the way it was in this county this time of year and year after year.

The weather had never occurred to Jerry. It didn't matter to a park ranger. He knew Mrs. Dean was amused.

Quickly, as soon as the widow took her eyes off Jerry and onto her plate, there followed a loud pounding at the door and windows that stunned them all and sent all eyes to end of the far corner wall where the wind and rain pounded. Even the widow's pounding heart slowed. The wind and rain forced submission. It was something that changed minds quickly and something to be frightened about. And as if in acknowledgement they looked at the door and windows because of the wind and rain, trying hard not to think the worst. Jerry hurried seeking the source of the pounding and swung the door open and scared them all. And before any one could move or speak, Mitch Field apologized for interrupting but told them a boat was waiting to evacuate them because of the storm.

"You won't be sleeping here tonight," he looked from the widow to Rose and Jerry, not showing a great deal of patience for misgivings or conversation.

Mitch led the widow out. Jerry and Rose followed his lead to a waiting twenty-seven foot fishing cruiser, with Latt Nowry from the fire department at the helm. Before taking the job at the fire department, Latt had done two tours in Iraq so he had seen lots of bad things, but somehow never tired of helping others in danger. He had a way of doing his best but seldom talked about such things like the rough lake water and thunder. It took courage to cross the lake. No one knew the best or the worst; whether to head to the tavern and nearest location or to head across the turbulent undercurrent to the church.

"Why the tavern, of course. Who'd venture further in this wind and water." The widow cast a side long glance at Latt that explained what she wanted. She couldn't risk going to the church because she knew the minister would be there. With all the bad weather, he might be itching for something good to do like marrying Jerry and Rose. A few days after the storm, every body would be replacing windows, doors and furnishings and getting home and cleaning up and not thinking about getting married, she calculated.

Mitch and Latt chattered about the home fries, fried fish and chicken. The best fried country food like no other could be had at the tavern. Nothing like weathering a storm surrounded by good country food and spirits eaten out in the back shack away from the women and children because that was how it was done. If no women and children heard or saw them then they wouldn't know what they weren't supposed to know.

The wind divided them and caused the water to get worse. Still on they went. And the young couple thinking of marriage, sat quietly together, though torn apart and turned upside down so quickly. No moonlight or stars, just a black sky, thunder and rain. A treacherous storm and unpredictable; a storm no one understood surrounded them upon this lake. It tossed them and the boat-not the ark built to carry God's children. A boat that could sink and never move again.

Up and down it went, bringing confusion until trembling, Latt couldn't stand a minute more, but smiled and went on with no safe end in sight. Mitch remembered aloud about many years ago and a thousand miles away to a land and a beloved woman who never wrote to him. In the night, Latt went on with the frozen figures glaring and listening to a man and a lost girl in the rain. He knew Mitch and the story and wondered why his friend told it. Guessed why; for him who had seen so much, intuition was hard to deny. Latt knew the subtle signs and lamented, remembering a time with soldiers, friends, trust and his boots until the dreaded announcement could no longer be avoided, "We must turn back!" Entrenched in the water's rhythm and the rain, he knew them and knew what to do. He wasn't bluffing. Turning, silence gathered at each end of the boat until the wind calmed and the waves followed. Darkness made safety impossible. He spoke to himself and to the vague distance as his eyes connected with the bright lights emerging from out of no where.

Jerry Bender uttered words of relief at the sight of an old rebuilt Mercury rescuer as sleek as a Chaparral. Aboard an exhausted crew included several men Jerry knew from the park. Rose watched him smiling with hope and the confidence from being in control again. Their path reversed, peril gone, in peace all hurried on to the church to the waiting crowd outside searching for anyone on land or water in need of help.

Tiring work for them all meant complaints about woes that caused them all to be ready for merry times that came from sadness because of shirts laying at tree trunks and dolls flailing on branches. The kind of things that caused the heart to yearn for good and joyful times with lots of food. The Benders insisted on setting a wedding date for the couple. And not even the widow could resist, "Yes," she said softly with them all holding hands right there beside Reverend as the deacons insisted with hope like the youn'ns playing tag in the moon light because they were children playing again at last.

Now some folks still talk about this story because the widow's daughter got engaged and some about the rather extraordinary journey in the rain and wind upon a turbulent lake, and the men and women being tired and half alive because they believe that's what really happened out there among those waves; some like convulsions for unhappy hours while Latt tried to make something good happen out there where it all happened. When the line between continuing on and turning back never seemed clear. When no voice came from the clouds or the water and no voice sounded louder than Mitch's that some other folks have described as mumblings. But call it what you will. Latt saved the people.And all who had wished, hoped, feared and doubted were moved by all of them.

The Boathouse

Patterman Winslow threw his legs over the side of the hammock and walked to the edge of the porch, his bare feet curled against the wet floor boards. His trousers were rolled up at the knee because of the water. The air was humid and the boy's curly hair clung to the back of his neck.

"Water everywhere," he mumbled.

The murky, grey waters of the Yew River, about a mile from the Atlantic coast along the North Carolina swamp lands had overflowed. Most of the farms in the county had suffered damage but the Winslow house stood high in the hills. The water level approached the porch and threatened to continue rising.

Maybe the water won't reach here, the boy thought. He resisted the urge to return to the hammock. Instead, Patt sucked his full bottom lip, turned the door knob, and disappeared behind the door.

The house consisted of three wings. The main section was furnished modestly with a winged sofa and matching chair in the living room. A big, black pot-bellied stove stood at the end of the room. Five ladder back chairs and the dining table were neatly placed in the middle of the kitchen.

A second wing, located in the rear of the house, contained the family's three bedrooms and single bath. Lastly, the attic, constructed high above the main floor so that extra rooms could be added and used as a playhouse by the two little girls who were forbidden to scatter tea cups and dolls in the neatly arranged rooms.

Ma didn't mind the play in the attic. "I know where they are," she said. Besides she knew the girls liked the privacy of the room.

For ninety-six years the house had stood in the hills. Each year it weathered the annual overflow of the river, providing shelter for three generations of Winslows. Grand-pappy Winslow, father and son, Patterman (named after a union general) had lived on the hard sod. Each generation had farmed the land, producing enough food to tide a family through the winter. In spring, the new growing season and the next cycle of life began with the Winslows always reaping the harvest.

It was a special way in this family. A close kinship existed despite the mixed blood-Spanish, Indian and probably Negro blood among the darker skins. But all were treated well and no one spoke about the color differences outside the family.

At the door, Patt stood thinking of his loneliness. Blake, the four year old beagle pa gave him on his thirteenth birthday was in the house, his leash attached to the fireplace to keep him out of the water, and away from the eels and moccasins.

Three days ago, pa, ma and the girls had left Clay. The family members traveled north to Taylor Town. They would make purchases for the farm and then spend a week visiting with Uncle Grange and Aunt Edna. Ma thought the trip would be good for the girls. They had just gotten over the chicken pox and the country air would do them good.

Patterman had stayed behind working the fields until the muscles in his forearms ached and his sun baked skin reddened and turned blue-black. His skin, when exposed to the sun, always took on this color before peeling in white flakes.

The rain came as expected and went on for three days, stopping for a few hours each day and then resuming until the Yew River and Black Creek overflowed.

No chance for the saplings this year. Beans, corn and tomatoes floated off with the water. The unpredictable spring brought clouds that hovered for several days, then it rained until most of the crops were washed out.

This year the flooding was expected to exceed damages done in over one hundred years. Some of the families had already left the county to live in shelters, hotels or to seek higher ground. Like the Crammers just down the road. Last night, they had phoned him, afraid because of the revised weather warning but he had convinced them of his safety. He hoped the river would crest but he also knew how to get out.

Momentarily, in a daydream, far away from the present, Patt pretended the water was receding. He turned away, walked to the table and switched on the radio.

"Hold on, Blake," he teased. The music of the "River Song" filling the room was suddenly interrupted by a newscast. "Residents of Tri-Counties are advised that a state of emergency exists. Please stand by for further details."

The water was rising. For a long time, he listened to howling wind. And when the rain started he rose, moving quickly about the room gathering food, blankets, candles, flashlight, gun, and bottles of water. By nightfall, he was ready to move to the upper level of the house.

Probably won't reach here, he thought. The old clapboard house had high walls and ceilings. Hopefully the water wouldn't rise beyond the main floor.

Once upstairs, the boy lit a candle. Electricity had never been installed in that portion of the house. A shuttered window was the only opening. He nailed Blake's leash to the floor board and then worked until darkness in its shadows and many forms filled the attic.

Neighboring Brady Town seldom flooded because of water from the Atlantic and the Yew. It was one of the few towns where stranded local residents and tourists came fleeing houses by the shore and ocean front properties and where the Winslows had come because it wasn't safe to travel further northward. Many people were in the same situation; waiting to return home, hoping for the rain to stop and hoping for a minimum of flooding.

More than a hundred people shared the lot at the Baylor Inn, where every body shared and helped after the hotel manager, Jeff Luddy, informed the travelers that the wait could be as long as a week.

"A week," echoed a man wearing a straw banana hat and holding his grandson's hand. "That's too long! Are they sure?"

"Well you can always go south." A lady standing with her identical twin said. The twins came to Brady Town each year for two to three weeks, and knew it was almost impossible to predict the weather conditions. Going south was always a good choice. The Atlantic was east and was almost always a bad choice. The man's chances were good heading South or West.

Talk of leaving and its inconveniences kept the population busy calling airlines, bus depots and local liveries. All the information created a network of information. About the time former banker, Phil Kilk, from Michigan arrived at the pool with the latest airline cancellations and skyrocketing livery fees from local companies, the Crammers left the lobby and headed to their rooms, meeting the banker at the pop machine in front of the pool.

With bags, the Crammers noticed no one but the approaching banker and he them; and he launched into his own brand of selling them the best way out. "North is closed. It looks better south or west...even east might be okay?"

"Oh no," Gil Crammer explained. "We just arrived from land just east of the Yew and the water's covered just about everything." The banker knew they had just arrived because of the bags and so much talk and discussions. He told them the Winslows were in the hotel without any news about their son, nor did they know the Crammers had been evacuated.

"He was left behind. And without a phone connection..." added his wife nodding. "Before leaving I tried and tried calling him but got no answer." It wasn't unusual. Because of the rain. But they knew Patt could get out. The three headed for the Winslows in room 211. The Crammers followed the banker to let the family know it could be more than a week before people were allowed to return. Patt was in the house and didn't know about the worsening conditions. It was crazy out there and it could get dangerous.

Tension filled the room. It was warm there despite the air conditioning. The phone disconnection riled both parents. "He should be here with us," Mrs. Winslow spoke up without hesitation, brushing aside her bangs. "Not in the house alone...it's no good." The girls hurried in from an adjacent room and watched, hoping dad could calm her down. But she stood firm, and assured them that most moms would be upset and afraid. She even suggested that her husband lead a group of men back to the house over the objections of the Crammers who assured her, "No one should go out without safety equipment and guns." Ma insisted, "Woouldn't you rather go get him...have him here rather than out there alone?" She challenged them all before collapsing in a chair crying uncontrollably, murmuring words not decipherable, but sensing something about saying the words was important.

The banker agreed to go. He said, "I want to go...it's gonna be tough, but at least I can do something…" The trip was like endurance training. "It won't be easy," Mr. Crammer joined in. "But we can give it a try...dam-it we can try," he said looking from Mrs. Winslow to her husband, nodding in agreement. Pa's face showed relief. His black eyes shimmered with hope and agreement.

Ma stopped crying as they readied themselves for the trip. The banker impressed her because of his many years of camping, fishing, hiking and diving.

His word and experience gave the men confidence. Less than an hour after the Crammers disclosed Patt's dilemma the men set out knowing that eventually they would encounter a road block patrolled by armed police officers or guards who would likely force them back and away.

Banker Phil saw the road block first; said he knew it had to be just ahead because of the barking dogs. Winslow spoke his thoughts, "Shit in' luck. Curse my shoe soles," but still insisted on forging ahead to talk to the three broad-shouldered officers, who would stop them with dogs and tactics; they'd do it with a little bit of kindness.

"Hi folks," the uniformed officer spoke to the three men. He'd turned back half a dozen cars filled with angry people and that meant something to him about his work. It wasn't play but he didn't mind it at all.

Winslow shook his head acknowledging the officer and explained, "My seventeen year old son is up near Clay. Have you heard anything?"

"We've been closed since late last night." The officer looked them over.

At the window he adjusted his collar thinking of what it was like to be seventeen as the banker asked about open roads heading north. "Not a chance," he answered. "Nothing north but water...and ain't heard nothing about a boy in Clay."

Phil handed the officer a business card. Crammer took a cell phone from his shirt pocket and dialed. "It's me," he said to his wife and launched into an explanation about the road block.

"Honey," she said in a soft voice from fatigue, talking and talking. "We got through to Stop and Shop and Bobby Reese...he will call us back. It's still a mess up there." Reese managed the store and knew what happened along the water. She promised to call back.

Phil turned the car around. Winslow sank into the seat thinking about how long it would be before word came about Patt. He contemplated it and stared out the window wanting to be somewhere else.

It was muggy in the attic where Patt lay tired on a pallet with Blake beside him. His thoughts drifted to his family, whom he had expected to arrive any day when the rain and wind came. Ma would worry. To her, he was still a boy. Both parents were strict about where he went and what he did. It seemed their efforts to control him ended with one of them shouting, "We do what we must, because we love you." Parents usually won that kind of argument. Just thinking about it made him restless. They would worry!

Maybe it won't reach here, he thought, tossing and turning the pillow again and again until he fell asleep to the sounds in the distance filled with hope.

Out along the river, sometimes water rose with a murmur. Or it came with a rumble like the toughest thing upon this earth and something told Patt. A voice entered his tangled thoughts, filled him and he awoke to a lurching motion beneath him as the wood weakened and the upper portion of the house floated into the river. He ran to the window and threw open the shutters. Water was everywhere. He had heard about houses being ripped apart by strong winds. Hurricanes sometimes swept away a complete block of homes. Unbelievable but the attic floated intact, along the river.

Excited, he untied Blake and they stood at the window looking for human shapes. But there were none. A flock of wild geese flew overhead. Swarms of flies, mosquitoes and water bugs dallied along the water. They watched the river and listened to the wind until the early morning sky darkened, and the clouds burst. Thunder cracked and lightning flashed over the top of the boathouse. Still four eyes watched until Blake caught sight of a dog threading water and leaped free of Patt's grasp. Two front legs cleared the rear window ledge. But Blake's hind legs never made it off the ledge. Patt grabbed him just before the final lunge.

No need to let him go chasing now. He didn't like to confine him but couldn't take any chances. Again Patt nailed the leash to the floor and plopped down beside Blake.

Boy and dog ate biscuits and ham. Patt swallowed the bottled water, almost choking. His mind raced. "Ain't this something." he said loudly. "We're miles from home..." He got up. In spite of himself he knew mental preparedness was the best means of survival. He had to stay calm.

Nevertheless, he was anxious and irritable. The suspense was tremendous. He spoke nervously. "No need to stress. There's no place to go without the house."

The mind again. He needed to think rationally. His life depended on it. Drinking water would have to be maintained. There were plenty of rain clouds. He could catch water in the bucket. And food. Blake could eat like a wolf when he took a notion.

"Rats." The words rolled off his tongue. Startled by the need to talk and be understood, he paced the floor wondering aloud. "There's fish in the river," he exclaimed walking toward the window. He threw in a throw-line made from an old hammer handle baited with a piece of ham. He softened with the quiet. The wind shifted, lifting the boathouse into the center of the river. Suddenly the blues and catfish leaped from the river. The current moved quickly. The line glided on top of the water just out of reach of the fish. He threw the line in another direction and noticed the boathouse passed near an island of land. A small band of people carrying bundles waved to him.

"Over here!" Patterman yelled, waving. "Help!"

Two men waded knee-deep into the water. Their steps seemed heavy and in slow motion because of the flowing river. The boathouse moved too quickly along the current.

"Almost rescued," the boy whispered, wringing his hands and backing away from the window. He thought about swimming to shore. But more than anything, Patt wanted to remain with the upper level of the house. He had to get it back home where pa could raise and secure it to the foundation. He glanced around the boathouse in dismay thinking about the rescue. So close and then the rushing water sent him away as fast as he had come.

It was better to stay busy than to think too much about being rescued. He had to find food or they'd eventually starve. The thought of starving made him afraid. His mind spun like the sudden speed of a boat. He sought the sky and saw nothing but clouds, like in the movies everything looked white in the fog. Like one of those days when the fog came in from the ocean through an open window. Unexpected, it crept like darkness, sending him to the window in unbelief.

From outside, in the white emerged the face of a man, about forty-five years old and with red, too small eyes or half-shut eyes that caused Blake to bark. Patt stared, not knowing what to say to this stranger who had come in from fog and water. How had he come to the house? And where had he come from?

As if to reply because of Patt's gaze, the gun and barking dog, the stranger grinned showing stained teeth and extended his hand, "I'm Luca," he said, hoping to appear friendly. One mistake could be costly; most men would have forced him out and away. No one was really safe along the water-but he knew losing his head wasn't an option; getting inside and staying inside for a while would mean taking it slow and talking easy to this young man.

"I can't take any chances," Patt shouted, sensing danger. Along the water few were friendly, most villains counted on deception. No stranger deserved trust.

"Hold on a minute. See here. My boat sprung a leak. I've got a heavy bag and don't want no trouble." The man spoke in a trembling voice, looked down at the floor, and raised his left arm in submission.

"Keep it low and slow," Patt said coolly. As if that wasn't enough, Blake moved closer to Luca with ears back and hair raised.

"What ya carrying in that suitcase?" Patt demanded.

The man stared at the boy, embarrassed by the question he wasn't afraid of this youngster. He knew how to persuade.

"All I own in the world. Don't want no trouble, either."

For Patt there was only one thing to do. Luca had to open the suitcase. What a man carried revealed a lot. There was nothing else to do and he let the stranger know it.

"Don't want no trouble..." Luca backed toward the window with eyes lowered and meant to avoid being shot or attacked by the barking, angry dog. "Can I leave my suitcase?" That would change his mind. It had to!

He fell silent and looked directly at Patt, who answered promptly, "You can leave it and keep right on going 'cause I know you can't stay. You ain't the kind of man that stays too long." Patt took three steps forward and the gun was less than three inches from Luca. This stranger hadn't deceived him. Leaving behind a suitcase was illogical, unreasonable, a lie and a trick.

"Sonny, something brought us together," Luca said heading for the window. He had to go but knew the land and water; fished, trapped and worked as a crop supervisor in North Carolina for many good years. Bad years in the hills taught him to survive and had kept him alive. The boy would shoot and stood alert and ready. It was a familiar picture. One that required caution and a prompt departure. Without a glance over his shoulder, he sat on the sill, threw both legs over the edge and disappeared without uttering another word.

Patt's mood lightened and he moved to the area just below the window. Blake joined him. He felt empty, thought of ma and saw her face. Real pretty. Brown hair fell in curls to her shoulders. He wanted to hug her.

She cried. He smiled.

"Ma!" Her smile turned to a frown. She shook her head and said firmly, "No." Her face faded.

Abruptly, returning to reality, he felt his body against the floor and rested, listening and hoping for a rescue, just as he'd done since drifting away from home. He fought the weariness. But remembered ma. By now she'd be worried sick. Probably had him skinned alive twice over. Then, not satisfied with the ending, she'd resurrect him and start over again.

That was ma. Cry and worry until pa stormed out of the room, so he wouldn't have to listen to her go on and on about "a man" who could take care of himself. Pa wouldn't worry. He understood what ma did not and accepted what was evident no matter how hard ma tried to change it.

He wasn't afraid; though tired, he sensed no danger and regained confidence.

Blake whined with no apparent reason but that meant Patt needed to pay attention. In his present state, he couldn't afford to ignore Blake's whining and nervousness. He stood up and discovered the house floated in water filled with turtles. Their once green shells were covered with mud and bugs. He had never seen so many turtles moving quickly with the force of the current. Rain poured, and blinded. Blake barked and wouldn't stop even when the turtles disappeared beneath the water or went inside their shells. Naturally, he'd rather be outdoors and in the water chasing them.

Patterman knew night was coming and at night the water would come alive. Gators, snakes and bears. He leaned out the window and drew in deep breaths of air. The noise faded. The turtles took no pleasure in their presence; most swam away following who knows what, swimming who knows where for food.

They glided along as the turtles swam away. He shuddered thinking of the night if a heavy fog rolled in.

White halls leading to white halls like stumbling around in darkness he told himself returning to the floor without the dog. Blake barked and paced along the floor in front of the window. He got to his feet and joined him at the window. His thoughts contradicted what he saw and believed.

A man appeared in the gray dusk ahead. A woman followed him, and then another one. The last woman talked on a cell phone. Patt wasn't asleep. Blake barked and growled with acknowledgement. No longer did the images seem in a dream or images brought on by exhaustion.

The rescuers cheered and the sounds traveled across the water. Patterman's heart pounded and Blake jumped on the window sill barking like a happy, pleading animal and nearly drowned the shouts of the rescuers clearing a way under a plumb full moon so that he could talk to ma and pa just like he had dreamed.

Mayion Creek Boy

Mississippi 1927

Louisiana whispered, "No," as she rose from the bed and brushed braids from her eyes. Dampness hung in the room and beads of sweat formed on her face. It was early, not yet seven o'clock. But she had to get dressed.

At the window yellow and white rays from the sun led her across rising waters in front of the house. Then on a quarter mile to the surrounding foothills above the waters of the flood, to the lush grass, berries, turnip greens and rhubarb.

People often traveled the water but stayed away from the foothills. So squirrels scrambled about doing just about anything they wanted. She imagined them happy and free running beneath pecan trees. Safe and far away from the water.

It had rained, again, last night. While Mama wasn't ready to abandon the house for higher ground, she wanted Louisiana to leave. The water threatened. And only in the hills would the girl be safe.

"Nelly will take care of you," Mama had explained. "That one knows how to handle strife." And it was true. There were women in the neighborhood who knew how to take the sting out of trouble. Yep, they worked hard at it too. These ladies didn't flinch in the presence of difficulty. In the community, everyone knew their names: Miss Minnie, Auntie Pearl, Big Sister Eula and of course, Nelly.

During the flooding this year, Nelly opened her door to families seeking food and shelter. Her house stood in the hills high above the approaching waters.

Most of the men had left the small Mississippi town of Carroll. After the layoff at the paper mill they left for temporary work at the mill town about ninety miles away.

Some commuted south to fish for the orange-red redear. Others went north seeking work in the factories or with the railroad.

"A man can't wring a living from this dirt," Papa had said before leaving for New York. "Hills can't feed a family and pay the bills. Going to my brother's."

He found work with the railroad. So this year, mother and daughter joined hands with the other women in the community.

"We're leaning on each other," Mama had said to Louisiana last night. "I think you understand all right... extraordinary thing about people."

"Louisiana Mae Ruffinnnnnn." Mama's voice startled her. "Your time has come. Got to go."

Louisiana ran back to the bed and pulled the sheet over her head, pretending to be asleep.

"Right now, get up." Mama entered the room and stood beside the bed. "Get up. Another storm's rising. Get dressed, now."

The girl lowered the sheet and opened her eyes. Mama rolled her eyes, sighed and continued; her voice trembled, "You've got to go before the rain comes again."

Tears settled at the corners of Louisiana's slanted brown eyes and trickled down her heart-shaped face. She nodded then launched her complaint. "You can use my help around here. I'm almost fifteen and old enough to help."

But the woman threw her head back and said firmly, "No, you must go." She looked into the distance, confused about what to do next and prayed. It wasn't the Sabbath but mama asked for help.

The girl knew she wouldn't change her mind. There was something about uncertainty and the water. Mama had good reason to ask for help. The decision was final.

"I don't want to go," Louisiana said rising from the bed.

"There's nothing else to say," Mama came back. "It's over and finished."

Louisiana stopped whining. Since the rains, mama had packed boxes of clothing and can goods. Furniture and appliances had been taken to the attic, far above the waters.

Now that another storm threatened the house, it seemed that the sooner she left, the better. Her departure would ease mama's load. With the hills just about a hundred feet from the house, Mama could escape. In the rain and darkness she could race through the hills without worrying about Louisiana's safety.

Louisiana walked to the bathroom and threw water on her face and hair while watching mama's reflection in the mirror. She saw her stuff clothes in a back sack and then start toward the bathroom.

"Come on...And don't forget your toothbrush," she said thrusting the sack in front of her daughter. "Let's go," she insisted.

They walked down the steps to the back door. Mama hugged Louisiana and broke the silence. "Think you're grown-up. Can do this and that and know it all. I'm doing what's right...and best for you."

Louisiana choked back tears and laid her head on mama's arm. But the warmth didn't take away the ache.

"Leave," mama said opening the door and shoving the girl across the stoop. "I want you safely at Nelly's before the rain."

Louisiana cleared the steps and had started on the path when Mama ran after her shouting, "Don't stop at Mayion Creek and don't take the short cut."

The girl ran in the hot sun. The air was clammy and her shoulders and back ached from the heaviness of the bag. A raccoon ran across the path. Startled, her heart leaped.

She wondered, is he leaving home because of the storm.

The sky turned gray and wind rustled the leaves overhead. She slowed the pace and rounded the bend at Mayion Creek. The water overflowed the bank. A huge magnolia's branches spread and almost touched the risen waters.

Louisiana felt tired and thirsty but knew the water wasn't good for drinking. She thought, running is making me tired and thirsty. There was no way to describe how much she wanted to splash cool water on her face. The water would help her aching feet. So she wandered off the trail toward the creek.

Wind blew her hair and sprayed dust into her eyes. She turned away, shielding her face from the wind but continued on the path to the cool water.

At the creek, she left the sack along the edge of the water, just below the bending limbs. She cupped both hands and lowered them into the water and fell forward. "Mama," Louisiana screamed, full of fear and fire. But her body sank beneath the water.

When she came up, the jeans clung to her legs and the shirt collar choked and tightened. Then her head sank again. Under water, she thought, the breath is leaving me for the last time.

Her thoughts came to a halt; she felt herself being lifted and carried away. Through the murky haze a spare face emerged. A boy about sixteen years old placed her beneath the tree, then rose to his feet.

He stood motionless. Black eyes stared at her and kept right on coming from a face the color of the clay in the hills. Coal, black hair woven into a single braid fell to his shoulder. He wore a plaid shirt and jeans.

Nothing about him frightened her. He had saved her life. Her body ached but the pain didn't halt curiosity. "Are you him from the reservation?" she asked but he didn't respond.

Sightings of this young boy who roamed the country side were talked about throughout town. "Do you speak English?" The girl reached for his hand but the movement startled him and away he ran into the woods.

Louisiana wished he would return. She wanted to talk and thank him. Here beneath the tree, she wondered again, and again, is he watching me. But could not see where he was or what he was doing.

Disillusioned and angry she turned on her side away from the woods and looked at the sky searching for its end. But could not find it. All was well.

A wind mounted and soughed. Leaves rustled and fell on her face. Tree limbs leaned and swayed. A branch snapped and tumbled in the air. The girl jumped to her feet just as the limb crashed to the ground where she had lain.

Frightened, this time Louisiana ran past the patch of wild flowers and loblolly pine into a field of berries. She tripped on an unearthed root but limped to her feet and didn't stop until Nelly's wide, screened, white porch came into view. A red overturned footstool in the yard had attracted crows. Being curious, they spent time watching the stool, stood beside it or cawed at it.

Louisiana felt sorry about what happened at Mayion Creek. Nelly would disapprove and be more than just a little bit upset. "Nelly," she shouted skipping between the rows of tulips that lined the path leading to the house.

At the sound of her name, the thinning gray-haired woman wasted no time getting to the door and inspected the girl with eyes flashing. What stood in front of her was muddy and wet. "Where've you been? Thought I'd have to send someone for you."

Louisiana explained the wet clothes and the mud. She told Nelly in an easy going way. And ended feeling lopsided. The right words seemed to be, "I was saved by the Indian boy."

"Did you drink the water, child?" Nelly's manner was cool. A calmness showed in the soft tone of her voice.

"Couldn't help it. I swallowed the water."

Nelly patted her shoulder. "Come on. Got to get you out of those wet things and into bed."

"I lost the back sack," Louisiana told Nelly. Just saying the words made her feel better. She watched the woman turn away and heard her say, "Sweet Jesus," before leaving.

A hand touched her shoulder, and Louisiana awoke. Nelly, Aunt Pearl and Sister Eula stood beside the bed. "You said a boy pulled you from the creek," Nelly said stiffly.

Louisiana told the story again. She stammered, trying to remember. Exhausted, she forgot what the boy looked like and couldn't describe his clothing.

"He looked like an Indian. But when I tried to touch him, he ran into the woods and disappeared like a ghost," the girl said. "He was seven feet tall." She lied but didn't know why.

"Are you sure?" Aunt Pearl started. "Could have been somebody just passing through. Too many tales been told about this boy. A woman on Viney Road said he ate on her doorstep. Then told Preacher she'd never seen him."

"I saw him," Louisiana exclaimed. "He came from the reservation." She fell back on the pillow. Her enthusiasm trailed off in a weary sigh. The lie made things worse and it was too late to tell the truth. They stared-looked surprised.

"Girl drank the water," Nelly said. "I'd better go for Doc Henry."

"The child is sick," Eula said. "Stay in bed. Don't want the other kids listening to your tales. We don't need the others running into the woods looking for an Indian boy."

"David's boy said he talked to an Indian in the barn. But when his brother search-ed the barn there wasn't a soul...just corn and an old tractor," Sister Eula added. She laughed and the lines at her eyes stretched to her hairline.

All three women nodded in agreement and then left the room laughing.

Louisiana knew they worried about the other children falling into the water. Everything had to be done to prevent them from sneaking off to Mayion Creek.

Still, she hoped they would trust her again and disliked herself for saying the boy was seven feet tall.

"Throw the ball," came in from the games and excitement behind Nelly's house.

Louisiana longed for the fun and fresh air. She sucked her teeth, closed her eyes and remembered sinking in the wet sand. The water felt colder than she remembered. Both legs got tangled in roots and rocks. *Her stomach churned and turned.* Then the Indian boy, with those dark eyes, set in that spare face wrapped his arms around her.

Seasonal Favorites

A Christmas Story

The last day of school before Christmas vacation should have been a good time for snowball fights instead of dodging hail and wishing for snow. All the wishing and hoping exhausted one of the two boys, and best friends, one fair with red hair and the other, the color of a pecan. Struggling against the wind to the intersection, the wire-like one followed. The leader, a hockey player and accustomed to the cold, muttered his observation with an empty expression.

"Are you still sweating the snow," Ben kidded his best friend, John as they waited for passing cars at the intersection of Hill and Brown, where they had met and departed each school day since about eight months ago when his dad moved the family from Connecticut for a job in Littleton, Michigan. Located about twenty-five minutes northeast of Detroit, Littleton community leaders prided themselves on being progressive. "A Twenty-first Century town" slogan stuck after the year two thousand when the population increased by the thousands as many families moved to the town fleeing high rents in the city and embracing a community that advertised, "all are welcome, come and let's unite".

John, an African American tried not to show his unhappiness about the weather. He'd lived in the neighborhood for most of his life. After meeting he'd took

Ben under his wing, introduced him as the new kid, and let every one know that this new dude from Connecticut could play hockey. Something not taken lightly because the last year's team had ended the season with a 2 and 10 record. And John had guessed right. Thus far, the current season's record stood at 5, 0 and 1. That kind of record made Ben a favorite at school and in the City-County Middle School League. John was happy to be his friend, even though right now, he didn't want to be toyed with about the snow, in the face of clouds and rain and an unchanged fifty-fifty chance for snow. The weather man couldn't be sure if there would be snow for Christmas.

Christmas in Littleton was special because people donated money and time to the community. Without snow some of the activities would go down the tube. Not the hockey game. It had been played earlier. It was played each year on the twenty-third. Ben had scored two goals and he felt pretty good about it and the win, despite the weather.

The Christmas day celebration appealed to families with small children, John reminded Ben, silently. He had helped every year since the community project started and it just wouldn't be the same without snow. Street signs and poles dressed in tinsel looked a lot better in the snow. White streets brought joy to those who recollected winter where the sleigh led by reindeer assisted the jolly old man distributing toys to millions of children-at least that's how the story goes. Without snow the reindeer's work would be especially hard and there wouldn't be twelve snowmen and the ice skating rink at the orphanage. The children liked the snowmen-they dressed them up in hats, coats and boots and beards. The mascots grabbed every body's attention- where in the world was there an orphanage with twelve snowmen built by community members who worked a little bit each week organizing for deliveries of food, clothes and snow men that started as early as six in the morning on Christmas day.

Something hurt in John's stomach. Snow was every thing and without it Christmas wouldn't be quite the same. It would be down right sad and that was the truth of it. "Did ya' hear me," Ben nudged John, grinning. "Snow's important but it's not important enough to forget the real deal." John listened knowing Ben meant to help. The two friends stopped beside the street sign without speaking. They agreed with palm slaps followed by double fist bumps that signaled their good-byes. They seldom spoke the words when departing. Ben turned eastward toward home and John went on straight ahead to the west.

John splashed water not caring where his shoes landed along the familiar sidewalk. Bushes lined the houses where sparkling clean windows revealed white vertical blinds and glistening decorated evergreen trees. Four minutes early, because of the rain, he had hurried and not minded, or noticed the time. Inside Mom, nodded her surprise and approval, wrapping presents for the church service, talking aloud about the Christmas turkey. Above the T.V. came her reproach, "Take those boots off." Her careful eyes never seemed to miss a situation for letting him know what she wanted him to do.

This year the family gave back to the church and community. They gave money and volunteered to spend the day helping others. A small gift exchange bought or made forced every one to work hard with the camcorder running and even harder later sitting and watching it being done.

Mom's special gift was a rhubarb pie; every one in the family knew she made one for the minister each year but didn't know this year about the second one for the family. The older, Lil, kneaded dough and seasoned fillings for the pie contest and didn't bother to look up at her younger brother. Busy and excited, she mumbled acknowledging his entrance. A distraction might cause a mistake and mistakes were hard to cure.

Dad napped in his easy chair in front of the T.V. with a blanket wrapped around his right ankle. The one he hurt jogging. What a sight he was with the newspaper he'd been reading neatly folded on the floor beside the chair. The family dog, Taffey, and the cat, Marble slept on the newspaper; the paper suggested something important to both the dog and cat because neither awoke to greet John.

Like most brooding boys, he lingered just enough to figure out what was going on and ran off to his room. Magazines and DVDs covered the floor. He counted five shirts and four sweaters on the chair in the corner and pulled three pairs of jeans from beneath his bed, making good on his promise to keep his room clean. The agreement with mom and dad had been made in the summer when they brought a home lab for him. It was a surprise because of his good grades-something his parents did because their own parents had done the same for similar milestones like good grades or helping around the house and at school without being asked.

He talked to himself and worked. Jars lined all his shelves and windows. He counted fifty mason jars filled with insects from ants to butterflies and bees. One hundred petri dishes made up a prized collection of molds from the kitchen. He counted the molds and reflected. Bread mold in the earliest stages looked harmless like peach fuzz. The worst examples looked like pudding and came from the school cafeteria-and more than half his specimens came from there. Miss Lottie, the head cook, had given him what was in his opinion the best specimen of all-a jarful of rotten eggs. After about three days in his room, mom and dad had protested. His prized specimen made every one sick. Knowing what they wouldn't tolerate, it went into the garbage disposal. With undisputed delight, he wondered what the eggs would look like now, after all these months.

"Gross vomit," he muttered aloud, finding a place on the shelf for his last jar of red ants in front of the two perfume bottles, one for mom and the other one for Lil; and a Lincoln half-dollar carved from wood for dad. All gifts made at school-each one unique and hand crafted. He slid across the carpet in his socks and out the door heading for the kitchen. Holding the banister, he took the steps two at a time arriving for Lil's imagined dressed up leftover chicken pie. She dressed it up with carrots and potatoes for the evening meal. But no pie for dessert. They filled the refrigerator and that meant hands off. That was Lil's rule. Christmas day seemed so far away-leftovers had that kind of effect. The room fell silent. Mom called to dad. He relinquished his chair at last, but not before inquiring about the leftovers because for him leftovers didn't mean much at all. Except maybe his speediest blessing for all who had to eat them, he always gave the blessing. He ate small bites before leaving his place at the table for the chair and a jelly-roll dessert. Mom laughed that a grown man could show such disdain for leftovers. Dad reminded them all that he worked half a day on Christmas Eve. That fact figured prominently in his lack of satisfaction, because with the recent lay-offs, every one worked harder.

After supper, Lil refused all house work which meant John vacuumed the floor. Two times over near the tree. Taffey and Marble ran away from the vacuum cleaner. He pressed on past dad snoring and napping in the chair. Boxes topped the trash can and it looked funny like, over stuffed and darker in the kitchen corner. He lifted it and held on. Outside, fog mingled with sleet and he hoped knowing that every one in Littleton wished for snow.

That night, falling asleep seemed like following a trail to no where. His stomach felt empty. It felt as though, he was walking around aimlessly.

On the twenty-fourth, John awoke to the sound of wind at his window and knew it was going to be another long day. He watched T.V. and ate cereal in bed from the private stash kept in his room. The milk kept cold in the window alongside cheese, an apple and a pear. All hid from mom's watchful eyes by curtains, mason jars and petri dishes. He nearly forgot about taking Taffey for a walk, but arrived in time to find him whining in front of the door with Marble slapping at his tail.

Outside, Taffey sniffed at worms in his path before running off after a squirrel. John walked from habit. At the corner, newsstand the headline blared, "No snow for Christmas." His stomach tightened and turned and twisted so that he suddenly turned and started for home. Taffey seemed to sense something about his friend's dismay and followed closely.

The sun shone along the grass as they scrambled up the steps. Seeing his sadness, Mom engaged him and cut him a piece of cherry pie still hot from the oven. She talked of family. Her brother, Tom, lived in New York. Her mom and dad had moved to Florida three years ago after the doctor insisted the warm climate would be better for arthritis.

Dad came home early and just in time to help Mom remember the name of his first and favorite bicycle-the one given to him by his favorite aunt who now resided in a nursing home in West Memphis, Tennessee.

"Bullfrog, I called it," Daddy explained. "I had a friend… we all called him Frog because he had such long legs. So I named the bike, Bullfrog!"

Ma couldn't remember and changed the subject because Dad couldn't believe that she'd forgotten his bike's name. An admission that allowed her no escape from his teasing even while knocking off a piece of pie, his sweet tooth ignored momentarily by an often too fretful wife used to hiding cookies, cake and candy whenever she needed to. Lil came in from the store dripping rain and shivering. She jumped in to help mom with a counter attack, "Too much work and not lack of memory is the reason for mom's forgetfulness."

John watched and listened without taking sides and earned another slice of pie. Lil wouldn't let dad get away with his teasing about mom's memory. She phoned his sister, Marie in San Jose. "Who is Bullfrog, Marie?" Lil wouldn't give up.

Marie came back with loud, excited laughter, "Isn't that one of the cartoon characters on T.V.!" She'd denied knowing Bullfrog and Frog. It was three against one when John went upstairs thinking of Christmas morning. Memories filled his thoughts. He heard mom's laughter again and again. He counted it dozens of times before falling asleep.

Dad called out to him during the night. Mom shouted, "It's snowing!" But he couldn't leave his bed. He listened but followed the stars and the moon carried along by the sound of a truck and its plow. The trail ended at the porch light. Taffey awoke him barking and pacing along the bed-he pulled the covers from the bed, "Come!"

John, up on the edge of the mattress with eyes half opened, saw the shadow on the wall. Snow on the limbs made the squirrel and bird walk awkwardly; not like walking on carpet, more like walking on eggs. He jumped up, looking through the window; his eyes met the snow man's at the edge of the sidewalk where dad stood deep in snow adding dentures to the snow man with the help of Mr. Goodman, the truck driver with the plow who helped out in the neighborhood every winter.

Another pair of hands would come in handy. John put on his rebelling jeans at the window and called out to them but couldn't be sure they heard him above the sound of the plow. Above his head white flakes tumbled and sparkled. He hurried, his thoughts moved through the air in the distance among the tumbling snow flakes.

With Elm

Persuasion often has everything to do with wanting something, especially when the voice is a familiar one. And it's not easy to ignore when a trusted friend, like Eleanor Northridge, Elm for short, does the talking. And I always listened because she radiated intelligence and expressed drive and confidence in every way imaginable. And despite what she hoped to achieve or become in this world, Elm's a got potential lady. A girl friend with striking features, bangs and a pony tail that hung just below her waist line; one who dreamed of doing impossible things like going to the moon. And one who once wrote a children's book about snails for her nephew, Kyle.

Despite the good looks and intelligence, her actions and attitude translated into words, "No shit," or "It doesn't matter." She was the kind of friend that I could tell anything. I once told her, "I wouldn't mind going out with my ex-boy friend's brother." Exactly what I wanted and needed to say after my ex- walked out on me for the third time, but still called every day to talk while his new girlfriend's son cried in the background.

Having Elm meant knowing someone who listened and wanted to change the world and even considered helping me get even with my ex- unaffected by what repercussions our strong wills might attract. And no, we didn't slash his tires or do anything crazy, but we sure talked about doing it. And when I called his new love interest to let her know he called me, his ex- daily, Elm took over and talked while we listened; the right thing to do to help a girlfriend two years younger.

It was also because Elm was stubborn and opinionated. Yet she was friendly enough to tell jokes to get people to laugh when someone said, "Hey, you look like a model. Are you Taylor or Tammie what's her name?" Not a bad thing at all, being a model that is. But it wasn't for Elm.

"What do they know," she often reminded me.

"Nothing at all," half of me replied because both of us studied English and wanted to be college professors. But contrary to what I said, I truly believed Elm should be working on a portfolio because that's what most good looking, long-legged girls did. And I believed that she should do the same, but never said it aloud in Gardenville, a town of less than seven thousand about four hours north of Detroit where we went to a small traditional college for liberal studies. So anybody going somewhere could be in Detroit in four hours. And those who didn't mind driving a few more hours could leave the state PDQ. Leaving behind Gardenville, we're getting out tonight.

I stood beside her feeling it never sounded all right to challenge her. And because she said lots of things that didn't sound okay and because earlier without missing a beat she talked me out of my apartment and into Wreggie's, the local café, because nobody stayed home on Halloween night. At least not Elm's friend. The homemade bread smelled good, not great. Nothing could be good about bread and deli meats any more. Any thing made in less than a minute in a room filled with the smell of onions couldn't be healthy. A small group waited at the take-out counter including a boy wearing a Frankenstein mask and a toddler dressed as a black cat. Their faces looked orange in the dim light where they gathered up black and orange colored eggs for a party. Like eggs colored for Easter, but for Halloween instead with lots of finger sandwiches made with black bread. One egg fell to the floor.

"Oh, Jimmie." A petite woman dressed in black tights and leotard exclaimed to a man wearing a mask like Zorro's. Jimmie came back, "Okay, Angel. I'll eat this one from the floor." He sounded annoyed. Her face looked like the red on the faces on children's watches. And it was more than the lights that caused her to look like one of those orange-red fountain drinks.

I am used to watching people, couples and crowds. Children too, and especially at the super market. It's something to do and always something to see. I looked about gloomily and the room seemed to grow larger and more animated filled with men's voices and laughter for they are the young, handsome seventies I had come to see. All seventies? That meant they all made at least seventy thousand a year. They were the real reason for following Elm to Wreggie's. And the only reason I'd drape my shoulders with a floor-length black cape exactly like Elm's. Brooms, cauldrons and wig-hats could be added later when/if the party got wilder and our capes needed accessories.

I wasn't sure what a seventy was supposed to be like but don't knock me for going out of my way to find out. Curiosity got the better of me. Remember too, Elm talked me into going out on Halloween night. And hell I just didn't want to spend another Friday night alone with my fifteen year old cat-the calico one I got on my eighth birthday and who because of her age seemed to be my companion of choice on most Friday nights-the only night I had nothing else to do. My aloofness and her age had a lot to do with it and there was nothing like staying home with an old friend and not going out with unkind people who zapped your energy, wouldn't motivate and inspire. You know what kind of people I'm talking about. The unkind and uncaring who listened to your sad stories and exclaimed, "Who cares anyway?"

But not Elm. And that's why I'm at Wreggie's on Halloween. I'm listening to Elm tell me about a car salesman, an athletic coach, science teacher and a computer programmer. All seventies! My mood lightened. Possibilities replaced doubts. There were at least twenty seventies in Wreggie's.

So I felt glad to be with Elm. It was better than cooking or grooming my cat especially when this really nice looking guy came over and sat down. He didn't even ask to join us, but sat down and started talking.

At last, a curious seventy had arrived. I sat still and listened to him talk to Elm. Then she contrived something about the moon, ships and the sea; some kind of story that interested seventies. He smiled nodding understanding. And smiled, gazed away and stood up and went on his way like it might be useful without a corresponding good-bye. Because of Elm's story, he left without a word and went off to a too thin, long-haired darling wearing a giant hoop earring. Poof and he walked away. And we didn't even know his name.

What can be said about a guy without a good-bye or a name?

So we chatted about regrets, got a refill and hoped for some friendly conversation and a name next time around. I emptied my glass. The smoke filled restaurant decorated in black and orange and a huge crystal chandelier all aglow spread orange-red-like sparks. Loud rap music from the radio rushed around the chandelier and up and down the dancers.

Elm slid closer to the aisle smiling and sipping rum and coke. She looked like a mannequin in that petticoat top and grinned across the room at the approaching men who smiled right back.

I had grown tired of creating and recreating something good when the two guys came out of no where and introduced themselves. One named Henry and the other, Wade. I wound up with Wade. He wasn't bad looking, but not as nice looking as Henry. Wade looked just under six feet. He wore a LaCrosse shirt; a white one trimmed in black. The black trim matched his dark eyes. Deep dark eyes that turned and paused.

As for Elm and Henry, they held hands just about one minute after the introductions. She really could pick them most of the time. He talked about his car. He liked them black and fast. Both guys liked bikes too.

The light of the moon crept in slowly and early. I bit my lip when Henry and Elm rose holding hands and Wade took my arm and asked me to leave, and we followed them just like that. He talked about his apartment as we followed them out to the front lot.

There was so little time to think about what to do. A small crowd gathered in the back of the lot where the sky was darkest, and where Henry and Wade had parked.

With them gone, I felt carefree and easy but not Elm. Totally struck by Henry, she wanted him to hurry back and said it. She smiled, more fascinated than ever.

"Yeah!" I lied because Elm would have done the same for me. What else could I do? I understood. I truly understood how important Henry was. Her eyes and words said it all, "Hurry!" She sounded warm and sincere but also very impatient and impulsive.

"They will," I said. "Have you any doubts?" Like nine feet long, I thought.

Six men or so crossed to the right of us and hurried to the back of the lot with amazing speed. Half a dozen rushing men came from the back lot and made me feel something terrible was about to happen. Shrieks came from out there where Henry and Wade had gone. Strange words followed, "Those two guys are towing their bikes with a hearse."

"What's your names," someone yelled.

The crowd in the back lot echoed coffins and Harley Davidson's. "Fire!" came from a shrill sounding voice from the edge of the crowd.

Elm started away, ahead of me. "Are you all right?" But not leaving me. The warning from somewhere in the crowd sounded loud and clear.

"Not so fast!" I found my tongue just in time to tell her my regrets, fears and anger. Our evening had turned into something weird and unpleasant. So weird that we ran back to my car, wondering aloud about that big black hearse and who owned it with dread. The kind of dread that comes from knowing something very strange had really happened and something even stranger had been avoided.

We sang along with the radio until the DJ's mocking laughter interrupted us.

What was so funny? Why did he laugh so long and hard? "Pandemonium was barely avoided as owners of Wreggies, Barry Jones and Roy Fields played the ultimate scary night for Halloween. Shocked customers were rounded up by policemen only to be told the whole incident had been a gag." I grabbed Elm's arm, but she shook free.

"The hearse and the bikes…" Elm couldn't get it out. The shock stopped her. High shrieks followed.

I pulled over and halted at the curb, laughing uncontrollably but couldn't ignore how crazy it all seemed. Click-click, events changed like in a movie. A full moon made me fall apart emotionally. My tears drew Elm's tears and frantic protests—every single tear accounted for.